Becoming Word for One Another

✠ ✠ ✠

A Spirituality for Lectors

Richard R. Gaillardetz, Ph.D.

ONE LIGUORI DRIVE
LIGUORI MO 63057-9999

Imprimi Potest:
Richard Thibodeau, C.Ss.R.
Provincial, Denver Province
The Redemptorists

ISBN 0-7648-0773-0
© 2002, Liguori Publications
Printed in the United States of America
02 03 04 05 06 5 4 3 2 1

All rights reserved. No part of this booklet may be reproduced, stored in a retrieval system, or transmitted without the written permission of Liguori Publications.

Scripture excerpts are taken from the *New American Bible with Revised New Testament* Copyright © 1986, 1970 Confraternity of Christian Doctrine, Inc., Washington, D.C. Used with permission. All rights reserved. No part of the *New American Bible* may be reproduced by any means without permission in writing from the copyright owner.

To order, call 1-800-325-9521
www.liguori.org
www.catholicbooksonline.com

Contents

✠ ✠ ✠

Introduction / 7

The Word of God / 11

Dabhar in the Hebrew Scriptures / 11
Jesus as God's Word / 13
We Believe in the Revealed Word, Not in
 Revealed Words / 16

The Lector Is a Servant of the Living Word of God / 20

The Two Tables of the Liturgy / 20
The True Nature of Scripture Is Displayed
 in the Liturgy of the Church / 23

The Procession of Scripture:
 We Are a Community of Memory / 24
The Proclamation of Scripture:
 The Written Word Becomes a
 Proclaimed Word / 28

*The Proclaimed Word of God Is Received
   by the Assembly in a Silent
   Dialogue* / 31
*Scripture Is Proclaimed Under the
   Presidency of an Apostolic
   Minister* / 36

Abiding in the Word: Spiritual Preparation for the Ministry of Proclamation / 39

Cultivating the Poetic Character of
   Words / 39
The Practice of *Lectio Divina* / 44

About the Author

Dr. Richard R. Gaillardetz holds the Margaret and Thomas Murray and James J. Bacik Endowed Chair in Catholic Studies at the University of Toledo in Toledo, Ohio. He has published numerous articles and authored or edited five books, including *A Daring Promise: A Spirituality of Christian Marriage* (Crossroad, 2002). He is currently a Catholic delegate on the U.S. Catholic-Methodist Dialogue and a past (2000) recipient of the Washington Theological Union's Sophia Award, offered in recognition of "theological excellence in service to ministry." Dr. Gaillardetz is a popular speaker at theological and pastoral conferences and is married and the father of four young boys.

Introduction

✠ ✠ ✠

As a parent, I have had to learn the hard way that words are important. I have four young boys, and they often demand that I clarify the precise wording of instructions that I have given them. For example, I might remind them that they have to clean the guinea pig cage, to which they would respond, "But Dad, you said we have to clean it *sometime* today. You didn't say we have to clean it *now*." Words are important because they are the principal means by which we communicate with one another. As we reflect on a spirituality for lectors it is important that we begin with words, for in a special way, the lector is the minister of the word par excellence.

When we use language to communicate, we do so because we desire to give something of ourselves to another. When I say to my wife, "I love you," I am not dispassionately reporting some objective state of affairs. I am sharing with her who I am *for her*. This kind of sharing of self is reflected in the expression "I give you my word." In this instance, *word* stands for my pledge of self to another. Words draw us together. They are the vehicle through which we make a connection with others by sharing in some commonly forged meaning.

Words are not just things, verbal tools that we use to accomplish some purpose. Words are intended to be uttered, either verbally or in writing. Words exist to invoke a relationship between two or more people. Imagine that you are at a convention with a bunch of strangers. During the break you mill around, sipping a cup of coffee, then someone turns and speaks to you. They make eye contact and offer a greeting. In that situation, you feel yourself addressed by another; you are the focus of someone else's attention. The words that were spoken did not just convey information, they instigated a happening, an engagement between the speaker and yourself. In this sense, we can speak of *word* as *event.* The Judeo-Christian tradition consistently employs this sense of *word* as constituting an event between God and humanity.

The Word of God

✠ ✠ ✠

In both the Old and New Testaments, *word* becomes a fundamental expression for the experience of having encountered God. It might help us in the cultivation of a spirituality for lectors if we reflected on this biblical notion of *word*.

Dabhar in the Hebrew Scriptures

The Hebrew term for *word, dabhar,* is frequently used in the Hebrew Scriptures to describe the manner of God's action in history. In Genesis God creates through God's word. We are told that the prophets hear and proclaim God's word to the people of Israel. For Israel, to speak of God's *dabhar* was to affirm God's effective and transformative presence in the world. The *dabhar* of God was not so much a thing as an event; it was what happens when an individual person or a community felt in some way addressed by God. In the Hebrew Scriptures, this event, this encounter between God and us through God's word, was no ordinary encounter. It was in fact, a saving encounter. That is to say, when they found themselves addressed by God, as Moses was before the burning bush and on Mount Sinai, they were in some way grasped and transformed by the encounter. Having been addressed by God's word, Moses was called to remove his shoes, for he now stood on holy ground.

We find this wonderful testimony to the effectiveness of God's word in the Book of Isaiah:

For just as from the heavens
  the rain and snow come down
And do not return there
  till they have watered the earth,
  making it fertile and fruitful,
Giving seed to him who sows
  and bread to him who eats,
So shall my word be
  that goes forth from my mouth;

It shall not return to me void,
　but shall do my will,
　achieving the end for which I
　　sent it.

Isaiah 55:10-11

For Isaiah, to speak of God's word was to speak of God's effective saving action in history. For Christians, this saving word comes to its unsurpassable term in Jesus of Nazareth.

Jesus as God's Word

This understanding of God's word as an effective and transformative event is taken to an even deeper level when it is associated not just with *a* word or words from God but with the definitive Word of God. At the beginning of the Gospel of John, we have that wonderfully poetic prologue:

In the beginning was the Word,
　and the Word was with God,
　and the Word was God.
He was in the beginning with God.

All things came to be through him,
* and without him nothing*
*   came to be.*
What came to be through him
*   was life,*
* and this life was the light of the*
*   human race....*
And the Word became flesh
* and made his dwelling among us,*
* and we saw his glory,*
* the glory as of the Father's only*
*   Son,*
* full of grace and truth.*

JOHN 1:1-4,14

This passage expresses the conviction that the same creative word of God, active in creation and present in the utterances of the prophets, has entered definitively and completely into our world as one of us. Henceforward, in the New Testament, the expression *Word of God* will mean God's creative and saving Word manifested perfectly and completely in Jesus of Nazareth.

In Jesus of Nazareth divine revelation takes the form not of information, facts, or even doctrines; revelation comes to us as a person. The communication of God's Word to us in Jesus is God's gift of self to us. In Jesus, the Word Incarnate, we are given nothing less than a share in the very life of God. This is reflected in the opening of the First Letter of John:

> *What was from the beginning,*
> *what we have heard,*
> *what we have seen with our eyes,*
> *what we have looked upon*
> *and touched with our hands*
> *concerns the Word of life—*
> *for the life was made visible;*
> *we have seen it and testify to it*
> *and proclaim to you the eternal life*
> *that was with the Father and was*
>   *made visible to us—*
> *what we have seen and heard*
> *we proclaim now to you,*
> *so that you too may have fellowship*
>   *with us;*
> *for our fellowship is with the Father*
> *and with his Son, Jesus Christ.*

> *We are writing this so that our joy may be complete.*
>
> 1 JOHN 1:1-4

This beautiful passage conveys to us the remarkable truth that in Christ, God's Word Incarnate, we are able to have fellowship with God; the Word introduces us into relationship with God. Only when we have grasped this profound insight into the God who communicates God's very self as the Word made flesh can we grasp what it is we mean when we speak of Scripture as "the Word of God."

We Believe in the Revealed Word, Not in Revealed Words

One of the things that distinguishes Catholic Christianity from other world religions is our understanding of sacred texts. Almost every great religion has some kind of sacred text. The Buddhist tradition has the Tripitaka. Hinduism has the Upanishads and the Vedic literature. Judaism has both the Tanak (what Christians generally refer to as the Old or

First Testament) and the Talmud, while Islam has the Koran. Yet there is something distinctive about Catholic Christianity's understanding of sacred Scripture. For Islam the Koran is a revealed text consisting of *revealed words*. The Koran was literally dictated to the prophet Mohammed. That is why, in Islam, the true Koran cannot be translated. The Arabic text is the only true revelatory text.

The Catholic Christian view is rather different. We believe that God has spoken God's Word throughout all of history. In the time before Christ, God spoke God's Word in the giving of the Law, in the teaching of the prophets, and in God's saving deeds in history. In the fullness of time (see Galatians 4:4), God spoke God's saving Word in Christ. The followers of Jesus would treasure their encounter with Christ, the Word Incarnate, passing on the Good News through stories, hymns, and collections of Jesus' sayings. Paul of Tarsus would write pastoral letters to communities he had founded, often exhorting them to fidelity in faith, chastising them for their errors or simply answering their questions. We believe that even though the texts of the New Testament were often written many years after Christ's death, they are, by the power of the Spirit, faithful testimonies to the encounter of early Christian communities with the living Word of God. That is why we believe that the Bible is the Word of God in human words. The words in the Bible were not dictated by God to the apostles. The biblical authors wrote in human words that they themselves chose from their limited reservoir of knowledge to communicate, as best they could, their encounter with the living Word of God. We believe they were inspired in what they wrote, not in the sense that the words were dictated to them but because the Holy Spirit worked in and through their own human abilities and limits as biblical authors. Indeed, we quite honestly admit that we have no original text of any of the biblical books. We accept the possibility of manuscript changes and new translations precisely because we do not believe in inspired words on a page that are therefore invariant. We believe, rather, in a living Word that was faithfully testified to in the writings of Israel and the later Christian apostolic communities.

> **QUESTIONS FOR REFLECTION**
>
> *Have you encountered people who have approached Scripture texts as if they were a set of revealed words, much as Islam views the Koran?*
>
> *What do you think are the consequences for Christianity of that way of understanding Scripture?*

The Lector Is a Servant of the Living Word of God

✠ ✠ ✠

This reflection on the meaning and power of the "Word of God" should help us appreciate more fully the ministry of the lector, for the true nature and purpose of Scripture is never more fully expressed than in the celebration of the liturgy.

The Two Tables of the Liturgy

One of the most important developments of the Second Vatican Council was its reassertion of the importance of Scripture as the privileged testimony of God's Word. Not only were future priests to receive much more training in Scripture study, but the laity were encouraged to study Scripture themselves. There was a call for more translations of the Bible into the vernacular. Finally, the council called for an expanded Liturgy of the Word. In its *Constitution on the Sacred Liturgy,* it mandated the following:

> *The treasures of the Bible are to be opened up more lavishly, so that richer fare may be provided for the faithful at the table of God's Word. In this way a more representative portion of the holy Scriptures will be read to the people in the course of a prescribed number of years (# 51).*

At the heart of the liturgical renewal encouraged by the council is the conviction that we discover God in both the proclamation of the Word and the breaking of the bread. Pope John Paul II's apostolic letter on the Sunday Eucharist, *Dominicae Cenae,* which he wrote early in his pontificate, speaks of the twofold table of Word and Eucharist:

> *We are well aware that from the earliest times the celebration of the Eucharist has been linked not only with prayer*

> *but also with the reading of Sacred Scripture and with singing by the whole assembly. As a result, it has long been possible to apply to the Mass the comparison, made by the Fathers, with the two tables, at which the Church prepares for her children the word of God and the Eucharist, that is, the bread of the Lord (# 10).*

And later, as he offered further meditations in *Dies Domini* on Sunday as the day of the Lord, the pope would write:

> *The table of the Word offers the same understanding of the history of salvation and especially of the Paschal Mystery which the Risen Jesus himself gave to his disciples: it is Christ who speaks, present as he is in his Word "when Sacred Scripture is read in the Church." (# 39).*

This insight into the nature of the liturgy is reflected in contemporary liturgical furnishings in which the *ambo* is often constructed in the form of the table, suggesting that we come to be fed at both the table of the Word, the *mensa verbi,* and the table of the Eucharist. This sense of a twofold nourishment in Word and Eucharist echoes that wonderful story of the two disciples with the risen Lord on the road to Emmaus. The disciples gradually come to recognize who Christ is through the careful instruction in Scripture and then, when they invite Christ into their home, in the breaking of the bread.

The True Nature of the Scriptures Is Displayed in the Liturgy of the Church

Louis-Marie Chauvet suggests that the Bible is most fully the sacred Scripture of the Church in the celebration of the liturgy.[1] In other words, only as proclaimed in the celebration of the Eucharist does the character of Scripture as "the Church's book" become evident. Consider this four-part movement: first, Scripture, in the form of the *Book of the Gospels,* is carried into the liturgical assembly with either a lector or deacon;

second, this written text is given *voice* in the proclamation of the Word to the assembly manifesting this word as a "living Word"; third, the community of believers are nourished by this Word and are engaged by it, entering into a silent dialogue with its demands; and fourth, this Word is validated as the *authentic Word of God* by the presiding ordained minister who represents the apostolic tradition.

The Procession of Scripture: We Are a Community of Memory

When in the liturgy we process with Scripture elevated by lector or deacon, we acknowledge the importance of the *written text* as a testament to the "earthly history of a believing people."[2] The procession with Scripture reminds us that we are a people of memory, claimed by the inspired testimony of the people of Israel and the ancient apostolic communities. This written collection of stories, teachings, hymns, proverbs, and exhortations remind us that we do not simply reinvent ourselves daily, we are bound by a sacred memory that preserves for us our distinctive identity as the new people of God. To be a community of memory is truly countercultural. It goes against the two more common tendencies of our age—either to be immersed in the present without any attempt to draw on the wisdom of tradition or to withdraw into the past without any serious question of the problems and opportunities of our age. Memory is more than antiquarianism or traditionalism. Memory, what the biblical tradition refers to as *anamnesis*, means bringing the past into the present and engaging the new problems and challenges of today with the wisdom of the past. The liturgical scholar Mary Collins offers a wonderful reflection on this particular understanding of the biblical sense of memory:

Anamnesis is biblical language which was long ago taken up by the Church and recently recovered as liturgical language....We can perhaps best understand anamnesis by considering it indirectly. Anamnesis speaks about a distinctive kind of human remembering. In common speech we are more likely to talk about its opposite, amnesia. We are familiar with the disorder of clinical amnesia, a diagnosis given to name a memory lapse of a crucial kind. The amnesiac is not the person who has misplaced her glasses one time too many. She is the person who has forgotten who she is. She has lost her conscious awareness of the basic relationships that give her her identity.... "Anamnesis" and "amnesia" come from a common Greek root. The biblical and liturgical use of the word "anamnesis" rises from a perception that there is a disorder analogous to clinical amnesia that plagues the human community. To be human is to be threatened with spiritual amnesia. At the level of our spiritual identity we do not remember for long who we really are. Those ultimate relationships that give us our spiritual identity slip from consciousness all too easily, and we lapse into non-comprehension about our deepest identity.[3]

Without some kind of memory, our existence becomes rootless; we are forced to continually reinvent ourselves. More importantly, without a community of memory we are likely to be formed out of the stories and myths of the larger society in which we live, and these stories are too often stories of greed and narcissism, stories that turn sex into a commodity and the poor and homeless into unsightly blights in our neighborhood. The Christian community must be a community of memory, a community that clings to the life and teaching of Jesus as it has been passed down in our tradition as the one true source of life. As a community we recall the stories of our past, of Moses and the Israelites, of the prophets, of Jesus and the early Christian communities. We retell these stories not because of our interest in historical trivia but because we believe that the recalling of these stories makes the reality they communicate present to us now. These stories offer a wellspring of human meaning that we may draw from in the face of the complex issues and tasks that confront us.

When as lector you have the occasion to

process in with the *Book of the Gospels,* you should be mindful that you are holding aloft the sacred memory of this community of faith. You are a privileged minister of the Church's own memory. Through these written texts, you are charged with reminding us of who we are.

The Proclamation of the Scriptures: The Written Word Becomes a Proclaimed Word

Reading is an essentially private exercise. Proclamation is concerned with engagement, with addressing others and being addressed. To understand the difference between the two, we must reflect on the difference between reading a letter from someone and having them actually speak to us. The lector is a true servant of the living Word of God. When the lector proclaims a text, it is not just a matter of reciting written words on a page; the lector is proclaiming a living Word. That is why at the end of a liturgical reading the lector is not to lift up the lectionary and say, "This is the Word of the Lord." Rather, without lifting up the lectionary at all, the lector looks out to the assembly and simply proclaims, "the Word of the Lord." For in your faithful proclamation of Scripture, you have proclaimed not merely a set of words on a page but the living Word of God. The Scripture readings offer an inspired testimony to that living Word. Through your proclamation of the liturgical reading, it is Christ, the living Word of God, who is being proclaimed to the community. When Scripture is truly proclaimed with conviction, that proclamation can stir souls to gratitude, call sinners to conversion, console the despairing, and exhort those who have become lax. The power of the proclaimed Word is described well in the Letter to the Hebrews:

> *Indeed, the word of God is living and effective, sharper than any two-edged sword, penetrating even between soul and spirit, joints and marrow, and able to disconcern reflections and thoughts of the heart. (Hebrews 4:12)*

The image of the two-edged sword suggests the way in which the proclamation of Scripture can speak to the heart of our existence. As Lawrence Cunningham has observed,

> *This word is "two-edged" because, unlike the short hacking single-edged blade of the Roman soldier, its purpose is not to bludgeon but to penetrate. When the word actually touches us it can do so in a profound fashion. It will not happen on every occasion but it does have the potential to happen.[4]*

Lectors must believe that this kind of life-changing encounter is possible every time they ascend to the ambo to fulfill their ministry. However, for this kind of encounter to happen, the lector has to honor the dangerous character of Scripture. One common failing of Christians is the tendency to tame or domesticate biblical texts by reducing them to a series of tepid moral maxims. Thomas Merton once warned,

> *There is, in a word, nothing comfortable about the Bible—until we manage to get so used to it that we make it*

comfortable for ourselves. But then we are perhaps too used to it and too at home in it. Let us not be too sure we know the Bible just because we have learned not to be astonished at it, just because we have learned not to have any problems with it. Have we perhaps learned at the same time not really to pay attention to it? Have we ceased to question the book and be questioned by it? Have we ceased to fight it? Then perhaps our reading is no longer serious.[5]

A spirituality of the lector must be grounded in the seriousness of reading and proclaiming Scripture as if we were wielding a most dangerous yet effective sword.

The Proclaimed Word of God Is Received by the Assembly in a Silent Dialogue

God's Word, God's personal self-disclosure, comes to us in history in the form of an address. It is the lector's proclamation of Scripture that allows the assembly to receive this divine address. It is only when the Word of

God is addressed to a living community of faith that it becomes fully "word." God's Word demands a dialogue between God and humankind, and the ministry of the lector initiates that dialogue. Pope John Paul II writes:

> *It should also be borne in mind that the liturgical proclamation of the Word of God, especially in the Eucharistic assembly, is not so much a time for meditation and catechesis as a dialogue between God and his people, a dialogue in which the wonders of salvation are proclaimed and the demands of the Covenant are continually restated. On their part, the People of God are drawn to respond to this dialogue of love by giving thanks and praise, also by demonstrating their fidelity to the task of continual "conversion." (Dies Domini #41)*

I never grasped the dialogical character of the liturgy of the Word until I was invited by one of the transitional deacons (a deacon preparing to be ordained to the priesthood) I had in class to attend Mass at the African-American parish where he was serving. Matthew was preaching that Sunday, and he began his homily behind the ambo, reading from his carefully prepared text. He had always been an excellent student, so I was confident that his text had been prepared with a good deal of study and prayer. However, he was not two minutes into the homily when I began to hear an intermittent murmuring, "That's right," "Preach it deacon," "Give us the Word." In response to these murmurings, Matthew seemed to come alive. He moved out from behind the ambo, abandoned his prepared text and preached from the heart, spurred on by the response of the assembly. What I was witnessing, I later realized, was a dramatic enactment of the kind of silent dialogue between the proclaimer of the Word and the listening assembly that ought to happen every Sunday, in every community. When the lector, deacon, or priest have proclaimed the Word effectively, we should *expect* this kind of dialogue. There may be no quiet murmuring, but in the silence of people's hearts, they ought to be responding to what they have heard, hurling their own questions and reactions back to the ambo.

The potential power of this kind of dialogue is reflected, I believe, in one of my favorite stories from the Old Testament. You may recall the story in which King David had spied from his rooftop a beautiful woman, Bathsheba, bathing. Struck by her beauty, David was reduced to hormones and, following the conventions of his time, had her brought to him, whereupon they had sexual relations. Because Bathsheba conceived as a result of the encounter, David sent for her husband Uriah, summoning the soldier home from the battlefront so that he might sleep with his wife and cover up David's immoral deed. Unfortunately for David, Uriah refused to sleep with his wife in an act of solidarity with his fellow comrades in battle. So David had Uriah sent back to the front with secret orders that he was to be left unprotected before the enemy. David's plan succeeded and Uriah was killed. This is one of the more popular stories of the Old Testament, and it's easy to see why. Let's face it, this is the kind of plot line we can find in any number of soap operas today. It is a story of lust, manipulation, and selfishness. But the story has a rather un-soap-opera-like ending. After the death of Uriah, the prophet Nathan comes to David, and appealing to David's office as king and principal judge of the land, puts a case before him:

"Judge this case for me! In a certain town there were two men, one rich, the other poor. The rich man had flocks and herds in great numbers. But the poor man had nothing at all except one little ewe lamb that he had bought. He nourished her, and she grew up with him and his children. She shared the little food he had and drank from his cup and slept in his bosom. She was like a daughter to him. Now, the rich man received a visitor, but he would not take from his own flocks and herds to prepare a meal for the wayfarer who had come to him. Instead he took the poor man's ewe lamb and made a meal of it for his visitor." David grew very angry with that

> *man and said to Nathan: "As the LORD lives, the man who has done this merits death! He shall restore the ewe lamb fourfold because he has done this and has had no pity." Then Nathan said to David: "You are the man!"....Then David said to Nathan, "I have sinned against the LORD." (2 Samuel 12:1-7a,13a)*

Nathan tells David a story, and the telling of the story elicits a response from David, an acknowledgment of his sin, and a desire for repentance. One wonders whether a moral lecture or chastisement would have had the same effect. When Scripture is proclaimed effectively, the possibility for this kind of dialogue always exists.

Scripture Is Proclaimed Under the Presidency of an Apostolic Minister

During the Eucharist, Scripture is generally proclaimed at the ambo by a lector and either a deacon or priest but always under the presidency of a priest or bishop. There is more significance to this than might first be imagined. In our Catholic tradition, the priest and bishop are ordained to pastoral leadership in the Church. It is their responsibility not to conduct all of the ministries of the Church themselves but to oversee (the meaning of the Greek word for bishop, *episkopos,* is *overseer)* the ministerial life of the community, to insure that all is done in accord with the great apostolic tradition. As such they hold *apostolic office.* This is why the presider at every Eucharist must be a priest or bishop, not so that they might conduct all of the liturgical ministries of the Church but that they might *preside* over these ministries, insuring that they are done in accord with the apostolic tradition. When the lector or deacon proclaims Scripture in the Eucharist, he does so in the presence of a presiding apostolic minister. This reminds us that Scripture is always the Church's book. Scripture is to be proclaimed to and received by an apostolic community of faith under the guidance of one who holds apostolic office. What impact does this have on a spirituality for lectors?

It is important to remember that Scripture

is the Church's book. In the preparation for the proclamation of the Word, it is always preferable for the lector to do that preparation in a communal context. Ideally, in any given parish, all of the ministers of the Word—the lectors, deacons, and priests—would gather together to study the Scripture texts that are to be proclaimed, drawing from the wisdom of the great apostolic tradition as they seek to deepen their understanding of the transformative power of the readings they are to proclaim. This very practice is recommended in the introductory notes of the lectionary itself.[6] In this way the lector would learn to be nourished by the communal interpretation of Scripture.

QUESTION FOR REFLECTION

What are some concrete things that you think the church can do to enhance the effectiveness of the liturgy of the Word in our Sunday Eucharist?

Abiding in the Word: Spiritual Preparation for the Ministry of Proclamation

✠ ✠ ✠

Throughout this work, we have frequently alluded to things that lectors can do to prepare for their ministry. In this final section, I would like to turn more directly to this by considering the need for the lector to cultivate a sense of the poetic and to explore the rich tradition of praying with Scripture that is known as the *lectio divina*.

Cultivating the Poetic Character of Words

Lectors must be lovers of words. It is that simple. If they do not have a reverence for words and their innate capacity to bear meaning and transform hearts, lectors will not be able to perform their ministry effectively. Words do not merely convey information, they have an almost sacramental function in their ability to speak to the hearts of men and women and make God present to us. But this is only possible when we overcome our tendency to think of them as clearly labeled and packaged receptacles of meaning. In a technologically driven, consumerist society, words themselves can be reduced to mere commodities to be consumed and discarded rather than something to be lingered over and treasured. Consider the lost art of letter writing in which a short note lovingly written on a small card by hand or carefully composed over a typewriter has given way to the instantaneous communication of e-mail. The electronic medium of e-mail, with its intoxicating sense of immediacy, discourages the careful pondering over the words we might choose to express ourselves. Quick messages and memos fired off with little consideration, often filled with typos and grammatical errors, have replaced the lovingly penned letter. This digitized form of communication has created a regrettable sense that words are ephemeral, easily deleted with a keystroke. Indeed, e-mail has made correspondence itself utterly disposable. No longer are letters from our beloved folded and unfolded to be reread and treasured in private moments.

The sacramental function of words derives from their poetic capacity. In poetry we are reminded that human words can lift our gaze beyond the literal and conventional to the "more" in life and to God who is the source of all life. From the perspective of Christian faith, because of the Incarnation in which God has spoken God's very being as Word into human history, all words have the potential of bearing God to us.

At the same time, and this may seem paradoxical, the lover of words also knows that all words limp. They reach out to the infinite, to God who is Holy Mystery, and yet never grasp or circumscribe that Mystery. Our human words, and this includes the human (even if inspired) words of Scripture, bring us to our God while never capturing the divine reality. In their brokenness, in their inadequacy, like the love poem written to our beloved that still fails to bear all we wish to express, our words remind us that we are called to encounter God ultimately not in words and concepts, moral maxims and doctrinal definitions, but as Holy, Gracious Mystery. Yet words are necessary. Karl Rahner once wrote of the importance of human words spoken to the human person about God:

Hence words must be spoken to him, which are such that he recognizes that they are uttered by those whom he must take seriously, and that he sees that these words call upon him to decide whether he dismisses them as meaningless or strives to listen to them long enough in truth and love—till he understands that their whole meaning is to utter the unutterable, to make the nameless mystery touch his heart gently....Christianity needs such words; it needs practice in learning to hear such words. For all its words would be misunderstood, if they were not heard as words of the mystery, as the coming of the blessed, gripping, incomprehensibility of the holy. For they speak of God. And if God's incomprehensibility does not grip us in a word, if it does not draw us on into his superluminous darkness, if it does not call us out of the little house of our homely, close-hugged truths into the strangeness of the night that is our real home, we have misunderstood or failed to understand the words of Christianity.[7]

Even the sacred words of Scripture ultimately are intended to draw us to that spiritual place wherein in silence we adore the one who comes to us in Love.

The power of poetry suggests that part of the remote preparation for the ministry of the lector lies in the cultivation of an appreciation for poetry. Like many things, the cultivation of a poetic sensibility requires time and exposure to good poetry. Reading poets who explicitly attend to the spiritual dimension of human existence, poets from the past like Gerard Manley Hopkins and Rainer Maria Rilke or contemporary poets like Seamus Heaney, can help the lector become better attuned to the poetic sensibility of Scripture.

The Practice of *Lectio Divina*

We live in a culture that has, in many ways, lost a sense of the power of the spoken word. We are far removed from those ancient cultures that relied almost exclusively on the spoken word for communication. Oral cultures gradually gave way to cultures that developed writing, what Walter Ong calls chirographic cultures. That, in turn, gave way to the printed word and its typographic cultures. Already in the last fifty years, we have moved from an electronic to a digitized culture in which we look to digitized databases and the Internet for the storage and communication of information.[8] There is much to be grateful for in this digitized age of communication, but there is also an even greater need to recover some of the ancient power of the *spoken* word.

Even after the development of a chirographic culture, the medieval Church retained a sense of this power of the spoken word. An important form of prayer in the monastery was called *lectio divina* or sacred reading. Here Scripture or some other spiritual text was read with care and deliberation—always out loud. The notion was that the bodily experience of actually uttering the words with one's mouth and hearing them with one's ears allowed one to internalize the words. It suggested a kind of *ruminatio* in which the words are digested by the spirit through the means of the bodily senses. To learn a passage by heart was not merely to memorize it but to allow it to take root in the deepest recesses of one's being. One witnesses this even today in Judaism as Talmudic students gently rock back and forth while they chant the text they are reading.

This tradition of *lectio divina* is a worthy spiritual exercise for lectors. Certainly they will want to consult commentaries and pronunciation guides, often found in competent lectors' handbooks. They will also want to gather with other ministers of the word to deepen their appreciation of the text's meaning and its application in their lives. But as a lover of words, the lector will also want to prepare for the ministry of proclamation by finding a quiet place to utter aloud the words of the text with great reverence and deliberation, delighting in their sounds, in their poetry, in their power. Say each word slowly. Chew each word and phrase, letting them sink into your soul. Linger over the associations that each word or phrase brings and the feelings that they elicit. It is only when you have truly digested the text in your own prayer that you can offer it for nourishment to others.

Perhaps the most tangible sign that a renewal of the ministry of the lector will have taken place will be found in the gradual disappearance of missals in the pews. When lectors truly acknowledge the full dimensions of their sacred ministry as a proclamation of the living Word of God, when they take the time to deepen their appreciation of Scripture through communal study, when they cultivate a sense of the poetic and grow to love the transformative power of words themselves, when they pray over Scripture in the practice of *lectio divina*, our communities will be drawn to attend with eyes and ears to that which is offered us. We will go forth from the liturgy, like the disciples who were schooled by Christ on the road to Emmaus, remarking to one another, "Were not our hearts burning within us?"

QUESTIONS FOR REFLECTION

Have you personally experienced any way in which our technological culture has downplayed the importance and power of words?

Have you ever experienced the spiritual discipline of lectio divina? *Describe your experience.*

Do you agree with the proposal here that lectors ought to cultivate an appreciation for poetry?

ENDNOTES

1. Louis-Marie Chauvet, *Symbol and Sacrament* (Collegeville: The Liturgical Press, 1995), 212.
2. Ibid.
3. Mary Collins, *Contemplative Participation* (Collegeville: Liturgical Press, 1990), 55.
4. Lawrence Cunningham, "A Two-Edged Sword: Honing the Proclamation," *Church* (Spring, 1999):15.
5. Thomas Merton, *Opening the Bible* (Collegeville: The Liturgical Press, 1970).
6. *Ordo lectionum missae, praenotanda,* chap. III.
7. Karl Rahner, "Poetry and the Christian," in *Theological Investigations,* volume 4 (Baltimore: Helicon Press, 1966), 359.
8. Cf. Walter Ong, *Orality and Literacy: The Technologizing of the Word* (London: Routledge, 1982).